WALTER LOVELACE

AuthorHouse™ UK
1663 Liberty Drive
Bloomington, IN 47403 USA
www.authorhouse.co.uk
UK TFN: 0800 0148641 (Toll Free inside the UK)
UK Local: 02036 956322 (+44 20 3695 6322 from outside the UK)

Because of the dynamic nature of the Internet, any web addresses or links contained in this book may have changed
since publication and may no longer be valid. The views expressed in this work are solely those of the author and do
not necessarily reflect the views of the publisher, and the publisher hereby disclaims any responsibility for them.

Any people depicted in stock imagery provided by Getty Images are models,
and such images are being used for illustrative purposes only.
Certain stock imagery © Getty Images.

All photographs by Heléne Lovelace

Front cover by Heléne Lovelace
Back cover by Heléne Lovelace

This book is printed on acid-free paper.

ISBN: 978-1-6655-9274-1 (sc)
ISBN: 978-1-6655-9275-8 (e)

Print information available on the last page.

Published by AuthorHouse 08/27/2021

authorHOUSE®

for
Anita
Heléne and Peter

INTRODUCTION

I am not an empty shell tossed about on the indifferent waves or whims of God or the careless indifference of countless philosophies. I am the result of hundreds of meetings with ordinary men and women all over the world. My brain is the resting place for ideas and experiences sifted down through generations of people, myths and meetings which have led on to words, actions, habits, character and then destiny.

My wife, Anita, taught me something that you can't find in a book or religion. A total trust in the worth of living. Regardless of sickness, wealth, ability or intelligence one can live to the full without expecting any reward. People are always attractive if you want them to be attractive. I have seldom met anyone who mastered this attitude like she does.

Poetry has the power of getting closer to the real world. It is a way of replacing unnecessary words with core values. The poet Ernest Dowson expressed this with one of his famous lines: "They are not long, the days of wine and roses"

I have tried to express some of my own life experiences in LIFE POEMS.

Walter Lovelace Stockholm 2021-08-18

Contents

Celebrate your qualities

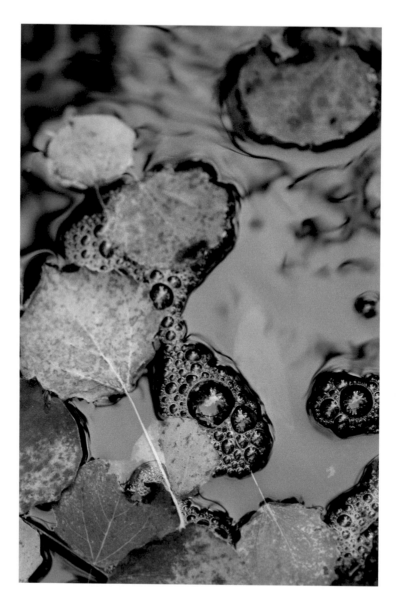

Springs of Adventure

We started a long journey
and made it an adventurous one
full of discovery,
full of experiences.

Mistakes and failures, they didn´t bother us.
We took them with us,
never allowed them to take over our lives.
Mistakes and failures,
never made us afraid,
they never put us down,
when we drank from
the Springs of Adventure.

We hoped for many summer evenings,
when with expected pleasure
we sailed into a new harbour
to find a new haven.
We hoped to see new places,
to meet new people,
to gain new knowledge
from the Springs of Adventure.

We remembered that the journey was all,
not the destination,
we would always arrive.
No need to hurry the journey
make it las forever.

On arriving we had grown older,
grown up into someone else
with all we had taken
from the Springs of Adventure.
And even if we were disappointed,
we didn´t mind.

Full of growing-up experiences,
we had learnt,
wisdom cannot be taught,
cannot be passed on,
only drunk,
from the Springs of Adventure.

Life stops when you stop dreaming

Yoga Savasana

Embracing mother earth supine
looking hard to find the way
Longing just to live benign
but stormy thoughts seem here to stay.

Imagine eyes like pools of water
left by sea tides on the shore
On the sand, they seem to falter
then disappear and are seen no more.

Imagine head and shoulders yield
limbs and body float away.
Nothingness is now a shield
and a refuge in which to stay.

Imagine that the mind is bright
as we balance on the razors edge.
Our goal at last comes into sight
no need now to give a pledge.

The burning truth is now ours.
Forever gone the wondering mind.
Now sharpened we accept the sign
that there is nothing more to find.

There is no answer to proclaim.
Asanas helped to make the flow
But now I know what for to aim
all Savasana means is letting go.

Hope ends when you stop believing

Quantum Particles

I am neither here nor there
It's really quite a lark
If Einstein and others knew it all
Then I am probably a Quark.

Higgins is a particle
That only lives a while
Where it goes to is a mystery
Into nothingness or exile?

I come and go all the time
On earth and moon and Mars
There are trillions of us in everything
Including all the stars.

Some say that consciousness is in the brain
The truth is hard to know
But Quantum energy maybe plays a part
To increase the flow.

It's all in the mind has someone said
Everything we see and touch
We make up everything as we go along
It really is too much.

My molecules and particles combine
To generate my cells.
And sub-atomic particles
Unite to make themselves.

Energy is what I am
Its not too hard to see.
That energy is in everything
Including you and me.

Live now, most people just exist

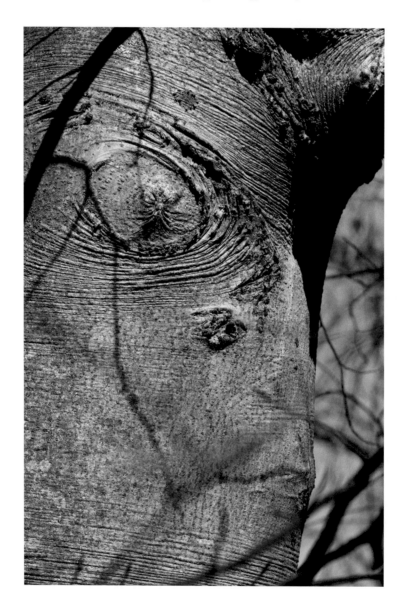

Alzheimers

Anita has a golden laugh to give
It could easily melt a stone
Alzheimers tried to capture her
To make her feel alone.

Music and dance are warriors
They fight to make her free
A laugh or a smile does wonders
To her sense of dignity.

Music and poems and photographs
Bring back memories to life
We must never let Alzheimers stop
This way to handle strife.

Questions are difficult for her
To understand you know
But just talk and take her hand
No need to make a show.

I ask myself the question
If God and Alzheimers are playing dice
There are so many of us soon
The odds are not so nice.

We can find peace of mind
It can never be too late
Regardless of sickness or of wealth
How to accept our fate.

Perhaps it is better to try
The art of letting go
If we learn this Yoga exercise
Which Alzheimers cannot know

Life is a beautiful struggle

Sailing is Necessary

We sailed out from Rhode's harbour
on a cold September night.
Our yacht was called Penelope
and she was nothing but delight.

My sailing mate was Niko
who was not easy to understand.
He had his demons to fight
I would know when reaching land.

We left Mandraki harbour
maybe famous for Rhodes Colossus
Our route was Poros island
by way of Nissiros and Kos.

We sailed out on a velvet sea
sheet-lightning filled the skies
A wonder to observe
and no thunder to terrorize.

Penelope surged through the night
under genoa and main.
Together we rode the waves
with flow easy to maintain.

Shooting stars passed through the heavens
a message from the cosmos.
Hope and fascination
so necessary for all of us.

Suddenly we were two yachts
passing in the dark night.
We waved Fair Winds, Fair Winds
until we were out of sight.

They say that sailing is necessary
No need to wonder why.
A look into eternal happiness
Seas and Winds will always satisfy.

A goal without a plan is just a wish

Afghan Boy

He came here to escape despair
and to avoid a sudden death.
Fear came with him of course
and sadness about the land he left.
He is honest to a degree
a pleasure to like and know.
He has his demons to fight I think
not easy, letting go.

He has done everything to be like you and me
he wants to integrate with us, belong,
Be self-sufficient and lend a hand
in that there is surely nothing wrong.
He is now a Baptised Christian
confirmed in this church of ours.
This is what he wanted all his life
when dreaming with the stars.

Politicians say he is not Christian
we know religion best they say.
One can stay, another leave
we have a lottery to play

The Taliban have made it clear
they want an Islamic State
Our Afghan Christian boy
must pay the price for hate.

Our politicians are not mad
they just want to make the news
With selfish hate campaigns
against Afghan boys and Jews.

Find your passion

Politicians

Socrates and Plato said explicitly
that democracy is not always free.
It does not cure corruption
you have to fight for it you see.

Politicians are not always trusted
it really is a shame.
They can say and do almost anything
democracy is just a name.

Politicians are never satisfied
and demand favours from left and right
These are not transparent to most of us
otherwise, they would take to flight.

Politicians sometimes make mistakes
and even when they do
They are quickly made ambassador
in Rome or Timbuctoo.

Politicians say we live in a welfare state
and equality is a must
They seem to forget that they are paid
ten times more than most of us.

Politicians can promise almost anything
when it is time to vote.
Afterwards they dare to say
that it was just a joke.

Politicians play the power game
morning day and night.
Letting them have their way
isn't very bright.

Walk away from unhappiness

Climate Change

All change, all change, it's time to take a stand
for climate change is here to stay.
For years and years, the scientists have warned
that we must change our ways.

The glaciers are melting
in every mountain range.
The seas will rise everywhere
it's really not so strange.

Antarctica is breaking up
in front of our very eyes
But bosses and executives
are slow to sympathise.

Carbon causes warming up
the seas and heavens shout.
It has taken a Greta to warn us all
that time is running out.

Our economies demand
expansion all the time.
No one wants to be the first
to budget a decline.

We must now pay the price
with a goal to which we must strive.
That we must change our way of life
or the planet will not survive.

There is hope of course
if everyone lends a hand
Governments and scientists
must cooperate in every land.

All change, all change,
we all know what to do
God will not solve the problem
Its up to me and you.

Respect yourself enough to walk away

The Best Life

Stars above, stars above
twinkling in the night.
Tell me where to find the best life
in the mountains or the plains.

River running free, running free
down to the very sea.
Tell me where to live
in the village or city.

Eagle golden, eagle golden
seeing everything from above.
Tell me where it is safest to live
in the north or east, south or west.

Old man, old woman
having lived in harmony.
Tell me which path to follow
and which philosophy.

Small child, small child
not yet tainted by adversity.
Tell me how to live a life
without harming natures diversity.

Where nobody hungers or is sick
where dictators are not allowed.
Where happiness is the meaning of life
this is my longed-for abode.

Life isn't about pleasing everybody

Hellenic Springs

This language of ancient gods
used to be All Greek To Me.
But my heart melted in the light
of perfect harmony.

We all speak Greek of course
angel, echo and democracy.
Gymnastics, ethics, physics
all sing a language rhapsody.

The pleasure of contrast
is lived everywhere in Greece.
Mountains, blue skies and seas
create a wonder feast.

Olive trees give oil, fruit and fire.
islands, gods and deities.
Olympic laurel wreaths
all weave the Hellas tapestry.

Imagine Socrates never lived
imagine the Greek Games never played.
Imagine Aristoteles never questioned
then Hellenic Springs are yet to be made.

Freedom is the Greek elixir
for those who struggle with the night.
Her ideas and philosophies
are a balm from Darkness to the Light.

Hellenic Springs have paved the way
for our culture to grow and bloom.
We are all Greeks at heart it seems
when Hellas plays the tune.

Printed in the United States
by Baker & Taylor Publisher Services